Psychology for Managers

Surendra Sahu

Contents

1. What is human psychology

   It is the scientific study of human behavoiur as individuals and in groups and in society. In other words it is the science of mental life.

2. Greats in the field of psychology

   a. Sigmund Freud(1856-1939)- 83 years.

He was an Austrian neurologist who became known as the father of psychoanalysis. He qualified as doctor of medicine in 1881 and carried out research into cerebral palsy and aphasia. He became a professor in 1902. He used free association(in which patients report their thoughts without reservation and in whichever order they spontaneously occur). He developed the Oedipus Complex. His interpretation of dreams was significant. He smoked and became a cigar smoker. He died of cancer of the oral cavity. His body was cremated in London.

   b. Carl S Jung(1875-1961)-86 years.

He was a Swiss psychoanalyst and psychiatrist who founded analytical psychology. During the world war II he served as an army doctor.

   c. Jean Piaget(1896-1980)- 84 years.

A Swish developmental psychologist and philosopher. He placed great importance on education of children. Before he became a psychologist, he was trained in natural history and philosophy.

   d. BF Skinner(1904-1990)-86 years.

He was an American psychologist, behaviourist, author , inventor and social philosopher. He was a professor of psychology from 1958 to 1974 at Harvard University. He invented the concept of operant conditioning and designed a chamber known as Skinner box.

e. Alfred Binet1857-1911)- 54 years.

He was a French psychologist who invented the first usable intelligence test. Today the test , after many modifications, is known as the IQ test. His parents separated when he was young.

f. Erik Erikson

3. Human brain , its structure and functions
Our mental life, our thoughts, our feelings are supported by our brains. Brain allows us to think and feel., to see . Brain enables us to do the things we do.

Thus the following adage is true. " Your mind what your brain does."Every physical movement, every desire, everything that you are proud of, or ashamed of that crosses your mind, will be supported by your brain. Our thoughts change from moment. With each thought different parts of our brain are turned on. Our brains are not unique but has evolved in some way from other species that were similar to us and far enough back, dissimilar to us.

Cells in the brain are glia support cells and neurons. But neurons have a soma or a cell body. Those make up the grey matter when we look at the brain. They have an axon that can be covered with myelin that makes up the white matter. The dendrite is the extension of the neuron that give input to the neurons. When you have a collection of cell bodies, it is called a nucleus and when you have a collection of axons, it is called a tract. We don't understand the working of our brain fully but our understanding now is better than what it was thirty years ago. The brain has 100 billion neurons and 100 trillion synpases, connections among neurons and dendrites..An average neuron may have upto 15000 connections, 1000 synapses and up-to 1000 neurons .Each neuron has the computing power of a medium sized computer. The time for information to go from neuron is 10 milliseconds
. The axons is the output signal of a neuron.

The human brain consists of the following parts:

    a. Cranium: It is bony structure that forms the head of the human skeleton.
    b. Frontal cortex
    c. Temporal lobe: These parts of the brain are important for hearing. In epilepsy neurons are firing and when they fire in organized patterns those become memories, desire, physical actions and thoughts.

    A 88 years old woman has a seizure and she says that she hears songs. She refused to take anti-convulsive drugs because she enjoyed hearing such songs..

d. Auditory cortex
e. Cerebellum: Half of all the cortical neurons in the brain are in the cerebellum. It is packed tightly. It is involved in motor control and in many other things.
f. Visual cortex: It is the part of the cerebral cortex responsible for processing visual information.
g. Auditory cortex: The primary auditory cortex is the part of the temporal lobe that processes auditory information in humans and other vertebrates.
h. Occipital lobe
Red coloured portion is the occipital lobe.

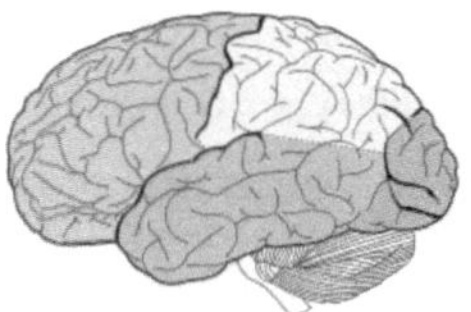

i. Parietal lobe
The yellow portion of the brain is the parietal lobe.
j. Frontal lobe: Blue portion.
k. Temporal lobe: Grey portion at the bottom .
l. Hippocampus: It is 2/3rd size of a thumb.
m. Basal ganglia: It is involved in movement. Parkinson's disease and Huntington's disease affect it. It is involve in reward systems of the brain.
n. Hypothalamus: It is the centre of the sympathetic nervous system. It controls

temperature, heart rate, blood pressure ,
hunger and body weight.

o. Brain stem: It controls heart and respiratory
    functions.

p. Spinal cord: It is along, thin tubular bundle
    of nerve tissues and support cells that
    extends from the medulla in the brain stem
    to the lumbular region of vertebral column.

q. Amygdala: This part is involved in fear
    emotion.

r. Insula: This part is involved when we feel
    disgust.

Basal ganglia is involved with learning-
how to be skilled at something. The
neo-cortex is involved in how to get
knowledge.
Medial temporal lobe on the left learns
verbal facts and the rught side learns
nonverbal or spatial facts.
All of your braan is learning , different
parts learning different things.

4. Mind
We humans are social beings. Brain is the basis of
our mind. Our mind is what our brain does. Our

brain is the physical basis of our mind and it is a physical-chemical system. Mind works at three levels:

    a. Cognitive

    b. Emotional: feelings, knowledge and desire

    c. Motivational:

5. Vision

It is how we see. The vision system has to overcome problems.

Humans can detect a candle 30 miles away in a clear dark night. The purpose of vision is

    a. Object recognition

    b. Navigation-getting around the world.

       We are able to recognize a person under different conditions of illumination, darkness or shadows., the angle we see at them, the distance we see at them etc

       Your eyes are moving, your head is moving, your body is moving and the world is moving. Still we are able to see and make sense of the things we see.

       Information enters your eyes hrough your retina- at the back of your eye; retina helps you to see the world. That information is transported to the cortex where higher level processing takes place which lets you know where you are and what you are looking at.

When we see each eye sees both the right and left visual fields. The right occipital cortex observes the things in the left visual field and the left notices things in the right. Each hemisphere of the brain is completely ignorant of what the other hemisphere is experiencing. The left hemisphere is the speaking centre. The brain is a society of semi-independent brains doing their own thins, sharing information as needed.

6. Consciousness
In addition to attention there are channels of information that sneak into us unconsciously or with minimal attention.

> Blind-sight: It is the state where people are cortically blind, but they kind of perceive some things. The world is divided into right visual field and left visual field as we look for it in the middle. A person who had a large injury in the right visual cortex was blind to objects in the left visual field.
> Anosagnosia: In this disorder the patient ignores what is on the left side of the plate. It is found in patients who have suffered strokes or had some brain injuries.
> A lady with this disorder is not able to perceive what is there on the left side of the plate and does not eat from the plate and also dresses on one side. They understand language and pay attention and for them the left side of the world does not exist.

7. Attention
Attention is the taking possession by the mind in clear and vivid form of one out of what seems like

several simultaneous objects or trains of thought. It applies withdrawl of some things in order to deal with others. If the word red is written in green colour and people are asked to name what colour it is written they tend to slow down. Some people are more prone to be hypnotized than others.

Attention is very limited. We can only process one thing at a time. Because of that we miss a lot around us all the time.

Bottom-up processing: If somebody throws a ball at you , you hear a scary sound that captures your attention and it forces you to attend to it.

Top-down processing: What is our goal? What are you paying attention top? What do you care bout? What are you up to? In this type you notice the things you are looking for, thinking about or you know are useful for your purposes.

8. Memory

Our fears, likes and dislikes are learned through experience. Memory disorders:

  a. Anterograde Amnesia: It is loss of memory to acquire new information, such as events you experienced or facts you encountered.

  b. Is memory in the brain localized or distributed? Karl Lashley had said, " It is not possible to demonstrate the isolated localization of memory trace anywhere in the nervous system..."The engram is represented throughout the system.

  c. Experiments have shown that non critical brain injury results in worse learning and memory regardless of injury location.

9. Learning

We use language to talk to each other. To communicate with others. We hear, we read and so on. The tone somebody speaks in , the tone you produce are also informative.

We are universal learners at birth. But we become enslaved to the language that we are native speakers of and listen to within months of birth.

For an adult the world is full of meaning, history, social interactions, everything that you are thinking about.

We learn in three ways:

a. Classical conditioning: This was first observed by Russian doctor Pavlov whoconducted experiments on dogs.   He found that dogs salivated at the mere sigt of food or the sight of the person brining the food. Even if food did not reach the stomach, gastric juices were released in the stomach. When a bell was rung and food was brought at the same time, the dog began to salivate on hearing the bell only even if food was not brought. If the bell was rung again and again and no food was brought then, the learning gets weakened and finally disappears. So you can learn something and you can unlearn something because oit is no longer an effective predictor of the future.

b. Operant conditioning: In this we learn to engage in behaviours even if there is no immediate reflex. People learn things by the consequence of their responses.

Law of effect says the consequence of a response determines whether it is strengthened or weakened. Reward will strengthen a response and no reward or punishment will weaken the response. In partial reinforcement reward is not given every time on an response but intermittently.

Behaviourists say that every=body can learn everything. It is nice when pleasant things happen to us but when things get worse, we feel miserable.

Delayed gratification: Here the concept is one foregoes an immediate reward for a greater reward at a later stage. One would like to do well at graduate school and later land up on a good job and foregoes all the merry making one could enjoy at the graduate school.

In the famous marshmallow experiments conducted at Stanford, children were told that could have one marshmallow or wait for 15 minutes and could get 2. It was observed that the children who waited did well later in life on all fronts like finishing graduate school, getting a better job etc.

10. Amnesia and Memory systems

Amnesia is the loss of memory which can be caused bya brain disorder or a brain injury. One author says, "….memory is what makes our life. Life without memory is no life at all. Our memories, our coherence, our reason, our feeling even our action. Without it, we are nothing. Our memories tell us what we have done, where we have been, what mattered to us.

Korsakoff's syndrome: The people who have severe alcoholism for many years develop severe memory disorder. The man is tuck in time. He very quickly forgets.

Anterograde amnesia: It is the loss of the ability to form new memories.

Retrograde amnesia: It is the loss of memories you already had.

Memory systems: Is memory in the brain is localized or distributed? /Although Karl Lashley believed it is distributed in he nervous system latest research reveals some ideas.

We have a symphony of learning instruments in our brain that empowers us to learn different kind of things.

Whenever a part of the brain is taken out in a rat, its part of the memory is weakened or disappears.

Hippocampus is he size of $2/3^{rd}$ of your thumb.

In one patient named HM when both the right and left hippocampus was removed his seizures stopped which had experienced prior to removal. The patient who had his hippocampus removed was able to remember anything for not more than a few seconds.

Repetition improves your long-term memory. hippocampus is important to form a new memory and it is necessary to remember a memory for a few months to a year before that memory becomes independent of the hippocampus.

Huntington's disease:

11. Language

Language give us the ability to talk to and communicate with each other and also lets understand what others speak to us. The main two purposes of language are:

    a. Comprehension: We can understand what somebody is saying to you.

    b. Phonology: It deals with sounds of language that we hear.

The brain has to reconstruct what is heard by the ear and has to assign eaning to them. By different syntax he meaning of what we hear completely changes.

Semantics is the meaning of words or sentences.

We understand semantics even when the sentence is complete nonsense.

For example, " Colourless green ideas sleep furiously."

Broca's aphasia: When there is a damage to the left hemisphere of our brain, we have trouble producing language.

Wernicke's aphasia: When there is damage to the right hemisphere of our brain then we face trouble in comprehending language.

By eight months a child begins to identify single words in a speech stream. After a year they can understand about 50 words. At this stage their babbling sounds like adults. Comprehension goes before production. The children understand words before they can speak. By six years a child learns about 10000 words. By nine a child can speak completely.

Girls on average outperform boys in language acquisition during the first two years of their lives.

Phonology: It is the sound of the words we hear. Words are to be governed by syntax and grammar if they have to convey some meaning.

The tone in which somebody speaks is also informative and not just what you hear.

Humans have about 100 phonemes across languages and any given language only uses a subset of them.

12. Thinking

Thinking is one of the highest forms of human activity. It involves problem solving and creativity.

Functional fixedness: One has a certain belief about what is going on and it is hard to overcome that to solve a problem in a novel way.

Whatever we do follows a standard distribution like a bell shaped curve over a certain period. Some days we great work and the next day we just do the ordinary.

We have an intuition about things , a heuristics, a feeling we have about things. We don't become a rational analyst and go by our gut feeling.

Anchoring: If we are asked to guess the length of Amazon and are told that it is more than 500 mils and then our guess will be different than when we are told it is less than 5000 miles. We come up with estimates which does anchoring with the information that is given to us.

The way any information is presented to us makes us think about them differently. Let us say that we are told that in a medical program 200 lives will be saved out of 600 people   . Our reaction will be different if we are told there will be 400 deaths. Although in both cases reality is the same.

When people think about gains they are risk-averse. If you are asked to choos between a payment of $75 for a doing a job and another option of having 75% chance of winning $100, people invariably choose the former option.

To make a truly logical judgment is shockingly hard, if anything, is a little complicated.

Frontal cortex of our brain has the job of initiating any action and has also the job of stopping it.

When someone asks a normal person how long is your spine, he answers two feet. But a frontal lobe lesion patient answers the same question as 12 feet.

13. Intelligence

It is a complex idea and varies from person to person. It is usually meant to describe the ability to solve problems, understand and learn complex materials , to adapt to the environment. And mental quickness. Studies of intelligence is always almost correlational and almost never experimental. Thus the tests for intelligence is subject to lots of interpretations and is affected by many factors of the world. IQ stands for intelligence quotient. The most famous IQ test takes about two hours i.e. the Wechsler Adult Intelligence Scale and is used for children.

It consists of vocabulary. You define words, similarities, information, comprehension. The mental age is divided by the chronological age and is multiplied by 100 to get the IQ score. 100 is the population mean in the United States. Raw score is your actual score and it is adjusted for your age. Score below 70 is considered clinically concerning. Reliability and variability is important considerations for any test. Reliability mans if the person is tested more than once the score should be the same. Validity means . means the tyest measures what is supposed to measure.

IQ scores correlate with GPA in high school and college, job success, salary, stable marriage, staying out of jail and how long you live. IQ scores account for approx. 25% of variation in these things. But various life events can be affected by other factors such as personality, education and culture. How much we are good at come partly comes from our genes and due to environment.

Flynn effect: It is observed that IQ scores where they are measured is showing an upward trend in all countries all the time.

There is the concept of intelligence about how a person related to others and it is difficult to measure this attribute.

Twin studies show that our genes play a dominant role in our intelligence. In monozygotic twins reared apart show a correlation of 0.7.

What is the effect of birth order on intelligence? The larger your family and the further you are down on the list, you have a lower IQ compared to your older sibling.The first born is exposed only to adults who talk him about the views of the day and all kinds of things. The second born has two adults but also has a older sibling. The intellectual environment for the second-born will be the average of two adults and a little child.The next one and so on.

A study by Hart and Risley who recorded the conversation in a family for one hour sgowed that the child's IQ and language vary according to the amount that the parents speak to their children.

By age 3 the cumulative vocabulary is 1100 words in a professional family, 750 in a welfare family. For welfare families the words spoken by a child per hour is 600, working class 750 and 2153 for professional family. The IQ you have at age 9 or 10 tend to be your score throughout your life. Some think that certain races have less or more IQ. We are practically the same genetically across various racial groups. It is seen that in the US in infancy there is no difference in IQ between the children of African American and European American households. Bu by age 4 the European American children have 4 points higher in IQ compared to the African American children. IQ depends upon the family environment you grew up in. We make stereotype judgments. Like we think African American are not as good academically as European

Americans . And we think in sports African Americans are phenomenal.

Stereotype threat is that others' judgments or one's own actions will confirm negative stereotype about one's own group. Is that we are born with a certain degree of talent or the harder we work the more talented we become?

There are a lot of things around us; we have to pick where we have to focus our attention. Attention is very limited. We can focus on one thing at a time. And because of that we miss a lot of things happening around us.

Bottom-down processing: If somebody throws a ball at you, you hear an unusual sound that captures your attention. It forces you to attend to it, because it is danger, it's moving and its unusual.

Top-down attention: What is your goal? What are you paying attention to? What do you care about? What are you up to? Things that you are looking for, thinking about, you know We notice some things and some things we do not notice at all.

are useful for your purposes, these give rise to top-down attention.

14. Emotion & Motivation

Emotion is driven by situation and adrenaline seems to amplify the intensity of the situation. Adrenaline is he neuro- transmitter that goes with high arousal. It raises your heart rates. Emotions can be cool or hot.

Cool emotions: thinking, language, rational behavior

Hot: there can be 550 different emotions like happy, sad, angry, joyful, anxious, nervous, mad. "That we fear , what we desire, what we enjoy, what we find disgusting—that all those things tell us what is important and whether it's to be avoided or approached, enjoyed or loathed."

Emotions are biologically-based response to situations that are seen as personally relevant. They are shaped by learning, and usually involves changes in peripheral pohysiology, expressive behavior and subjective experience.,
Mood is diffuse and long-lasting emotional state. Emotion is immediate response to a certain situation.
Arousal: a. high:
Emotion works in peculiar ways. In the podium of the Olympic prize winner, the bronze medal winner looks happiest and the silver medal winner looks saddest as the later feels that he could have won the gold medal.
Through facial expressions we communicate with each other. If you experience fear your eyes get bigger and with disgust your eys get to close.
Animals such as mice and rats, in which amygdale has been removed, lose the fear they ought to have of a cat.
Fear is a powerful emotion for survival and safety. We are afraid of what may ill us or cause us pain.
Amygdala transforms emotions into memories.
Insula, another part of the brain, is linked with

disgust. Women have a better memory of emotional events compared to men.
Adrenaline is the neuro-hormone that goes with high arousal. It raises your heart rate. Emotion is driven by situation and adrenaline seems to amplify the intensity of the situation.

15. Personality

Every person is

- Like all other persons,
- Like some other persons.
- Like no other person.

Personality is asset of behavioural, emotional and cognitive tendencies that people display over time.

Somebody is shy, somebody is helpful, somebody is rude. And across situations , not just one place, one time but pretty regularly. It varies across people.

Trait: It is feature in you that is constant across situations and times. It can be thought of as a continuum. If we consider introversion versus extroversion, it is not that everybody is one or the other, but many of us are somewhere in between.

Sate: How we feel temporarily; how do we feel, excited or afraid.

Situations: .They are specific at times and places and that influences us. So trait, state and situation may determine how we feel inside and how e act in the world.

In a Harvard study it was seen that the children who had control in their behavior did not get into crime when they became 21.

 Dopamine is the reward transmitter.

Introverts are more aroused in the morning and less in the evening. They tend to get up early n the morning. Extroverts are more aroused in the evening and less in the morning. One could be super aroused, super nervous, shaky, sleepy. Somewhere in the middle goes with the best performance.

In general men tend to be taller than women. But some women are taller than lots of individual men. The older you get the more consistent you become over a span of time, say seven years. As we grow older we develop habits and get set in our ways. We can gave introverted or extroverted personality. Social anxiety disorder can be termed as shyness. But it is tricky to draw a line between highly extroverted people versus highly introverted people.
Your tendency to be happy also comes largely fifty percent from your genes. Empirical evidence shows that parents and home environments appear to have nearly zero influence on your personality.

-Other fifty percent could come environment like diet or health. Environmental influences include education, parenting and everything else like religious practices.

Those who adopt good habits like balanced diet and regular exercise are seen to avoid Alzheimer's disease. Personality could be outgoing or not, agreeable or not, open or not.

Twin studies show that people's behavior such as time spent watching television, number of childhood accidents, tendency for marriage and divorce,,, religious attitudes, balance between work and leisure have a correlation of 0.5 that is about half heritable .

16. Child Development

A child's mind is fundamentally different from an adult's. Babies are thought to be cute. Babies have rounder heads, foreheads that slant back ore, have larger eyes proportionally and lower jaw bones. Baby-faced adults are considered to be more naïve, more honest, more helpless, more kind, more warm. The cuteness of a baby is thought to be an evolutionary reward for dealing with a baby.

It seems within moments of birth infants tend to imitate adults. Infants love to control. Or provoke , their environment. By five or six months infants tend to explore the world by their hands and their eyes around them. Infants who are little better at following eyes alkso learn language faster.

As a child develops two things happen:

> 1   Assimilation: One incorporates new knowledge into existing cognitive

structures. It is about the way you think about the world.

2   Adaptation: It is about how your understanding of the world changes through development to acquire new evidence.

Sensori-motor stage: This takes place between 0 to two years. In this the world is what you see and the physical actions. They cannot represent what they cannot see in front of them.

Two-seven years: In this stage you are able to keep a thought in your mind. You see the world from your view but not appreciating the views of somebody else. You use language.

Seven to eleven years: One organizes logical thought.

Autism is a childhood development disease. It is estimated that it is present in 1 out of every 140 children. More boys have autism compared to girls. A child wqith autism has the following defects:

a.   They are weak in social interaction. They have lot of repetitive behavior which becomes a hindrance id developing interaction with others.

b.   Their brains develop slowly and they are unable to understand the contents of thoughts of other people.

    c.   The mind development in these children are delayed by 5 to 6 years.
    d.   They have difficulty in relating to other people and understanding what the other people is thinking and feeling.
Children begin to count from a very early age ,s ay six months.

17. Adult Development

It is the changes in biological, psychological and interpersonal domains of human life from the end of adolescence UNTIL THE END OF ONE'S LIFE.
These CHANGES MAY BE GRADUAL OR rapid.
Changes occur at the cellular level.
An adult is a person who has reached the age at which they are considered responsible for their actions and therefore legally accountable for them.
It is 18 in most countries and varies from 16 to 21.

18. Stress

It is a psychological and physiological response to a stimulus, a stressor, that alters the body's equilibrium.
Physical stress: acute: Like injury
Chronic: hunger, cancer, long-term problems
Psychological stress: Acute: Deadline, humiliation
Chronic: chronic work pressure, isolation.
For animals in the wild stress is typically acute, and physical and is a response to something that happens. It is about the body's survival and then you act.

For modern people stress is often chronic and psychological. The modern man does not face a physical threat.

In 1900 the major cause of death in the United Sates was childbirth and infectious diseases.

In 2007 people are dying of heart diseases and cancer.

The sympathetic nervous system goes from the brain to the spine to the organs to blood vessels to sweat glands to muscles and hairs. The parasympathetic nervous system operates highly when you are asleep , or you're eating or your' relaxing. Cortisol is released within minutes when one experiences stress and it follows brain to hypothalamus to pituitary to kidney circuit.

Earlier it was thought that ulcers were formed due to stress and food. But in 2005 the research by Barry Marshall has showed it is due to the helicon-bacter bacterium.

PTSD(Post Trauma Stress Disorder): Those with smaller hippocampus are likely to experience PTSD. People facing stress , if have an outlet for their frustrations, will faceless of toxic effects of stress.

19. Psychopathology

Many of us suffer from some form of mental illness sometime in our life without knowing. Every neuro-psychiatric disorder is basically a syndrome. It is a clustr of things that tend to go together. The criteria for mental illness is changing over time and is enumerated in DSM which brings out periodically. Perhaps we know someone who suffers from a mental illness. Various forms are:

a. Schizophrenia
b. Depression
c. Huntington's disease
d. Anxiety
e. Bipolar disorder
f. Substance abuse(alcohol and drugs)
g. Panic disorder
h. Phobia
i. Developmental disorder like autism
j. ADHD
k. Dyslexia
l. Obsessive Compulsive Disorder
m. Anorexia
n. Bulimia

About half all individuals would have faced for brief periods some psychiatric disorder. It can be rare and devastating. Mental disorder is a clinically significant behavioural or psychological syndrome/ or pattern that occurs in a person and that is associated with present distress or disability or with significantly increased risk of suffering death, pain, disability or important loss of freedom.

A psychiatrist asks his patients can you lead a happy personal life? Can you lead a reasonably successful professional life? Some people think that mental illness is nothing but labeling that which we find unpleasant or difficult, non-conforming , or deviant.

The mentally-ill patients face misery and is shared by their family members.

Schizophrenia: About one percent of population worldwide suffer from this ailment. Earlier people did not know how to deal with people afflicted by this disease and labeled it as possession or witchcraft. Schizophrenic patients have unusual beliefs and delusions. They seem to feel auditory hallucinations, mood disorders and motor alteration. Schizophrenic patients show symptoms when they are 18, 20, 22 or 24 years of age. It is probably caused by genetic factors. Neuroleptics which block post-synaptic dopamine receptors are used to treat schizophrenia. The drug is effective within hours and maximum clinical effect takes weeks and the effect remains after the treatment is stopped.

It is difficult to develop drugs for psychiatric disorders. All the drugs used are by happenstance which helped the patients. Medicines have side effects, sometime very undesirable ones.

In 1940s frontal lobotomies were introduced which made hard-to deal   with patients easier to deal with.

Tourtte's syndrome: In this the patient has involuntary tics and curses in horrific ways.

Huntington's disease: It is a rare genetic disease and is found in persons in their 30s and 40s. These patients

get severe motor problems and movement problems
and then over time cognitive and psychiatric problems.
There is no treatment for it.

Alzheimer's disease: People above the age of 85 are
likely suffer from this disease. It is progressive
dementia, i.e. many losses of ability. Problems start
with memory but over time affects language, thinking,
concentration, spatial thinking , sometimes mood .and
personality. In Alzheimer's patients the hippocampus
withers away on both sides of the brain.

20. Social Psychology

Social psychology tells us about how we
relate to others. It is the scientific study of
the way in which our thoughts, feelings and
behaviours are influenced by the real or
imagined presence of other people.
Social psychology deals with the following
aspects:

a.   Self concept
b.   Impression of others
c.   Cultural differences
d.   Autism

When we think of ourselves we are
prone to self-serving attributional
bias. People attribute success to
their traits and failures to
situations.

False consensus: People choosing to
engage in a behavior believe that
their choice is more common than

do people making the opposite choice.

Attitude versus action:

The power of the situation: Are we inclined to behave in a certain way or Self-serving Attributional Bias: In this people generally overrate themselves. When asked to do both teachers and students overrate themselves.

our behavior depends upon the situation we are put in?

Fundamental attribution error: When other people do things it is their character, and especially failings are because of failings of their character.

When we do things we are not especially proud of or do not think are awesome, that's the situation that made us do that.

People are biased top attribute heir success to their wonderful traits and their failures to situations.

False consensus: People choose to engage in a behavior that those people who do that believe that it's more common and that more people do that, that when you do something, the more you do it, the

more you think other people do it ,
too.

If you see a lot of people throwing
garbage onto the beach, nto the
streets, what are you allowed to
do? You also throw garbage
although it is bad to do so.

Attitude vs Action: Although we
have a certain attitude but our
actions are not in consonance with
our attitude.

Conformity:

Compliance:

 Obedience:

 Bystanders and Helping:

Discouraging deviant behavior: It is
observed that in stead of showing
the deviant behavoiur and asking
people not to indulge in them , it is
better to show hem the desired
behavior in advertisement to make
them indulge in the desired
behavior.

Cognitive dissonance: There is a gap
between our attitudes and
behavior. Leon Festinger coined this
term where he made people to do a
really boring task like turning little
screws by a quarter and paid either
$1 or $20 for the same task to two
experimental groups. The group
which was paid $20 were asked to

tell the next person coming that this was an interesting and worthwhile task. Those who were paid more justified top them why they had lied about the task although they felt that it was a boring task.

When people make a choice , they rate it awesome, no matter what.

First impressions: How powerful are they, how valid and how accurate? When we do not like someone at first sight or have negative ideas about somebody for some reason, we do not behave with them as nicely and the other person also thinks negatively about us and confirms our belief. Thus self fulfilling prophecy acts in this case.

Cultures: Different countries and cultures also make us see the world one way or the other.

Autism: In children this disorder is found in one out of a hundred. In this disorder children experience difficulties in social cognition, communication and stereotyped repetitive movements. Children with autism don't have a natural desire to socially interact with their parents, siblings, their cartakers.

21. Evolutionary Psychology

We have evolved from a number pf species and the way men and women react to sex and pro=creation is different as the investment in child raring is different for men and women. Thus in a study where an attractive male approached women in a library for a date, or to go apartment or sex , the response of women were different than men who were approached by an attractive female.

Event	Women	Men
Date	50%	50%
Apartment	26%	56%
Sex	0%	76%

22. Positive psychology

What is Positive Psychology

It is the study of positive emotions and how e can remove the negative emotions from our lives.

Chris Peterson was one of the psychologists who did research on the subject.

Chris Peterson: We all experiences positive and negative emotions and we are bound give a response to them when we experience such emotions. Some people find it difficult to move away from the negative emotions. For a particular emotion different people react differently.

The general process of reacting to an emotion is as under:

Current situation~ Appraisal of the emotion ~Changes in face, body states, posture, voice, action urges; feeling states ~ *Response.*

1. Ten Positive Emotions

Positive emotions are subtle. Think of a situation when you experienced a good emotion. How did you feel? Who were with at the time?

The following ten emotions can be discerned and their appraisal, tendency and output are given in the following table:

Emotion	Appraisal	Tendency	Outcome
joy	Safe, familiar	play	Acquire skills
gratitude	Receive altruistic gift		Social bond, skills for loving
serenity	Safe, certain, low effort	Savour and integrate	Modify self and world view
Interest	Safe, novel, mysterious	Explore	Gain knowledge, energy, hope
Hope	Fear the worst, yearn for better	Be inventive	Increased resilience
Pride	Socially valid achievemen t	Dream big	Further achievements
Amuseme nt		Share laughter, insights	Build friendship, creative
Inspiratio n	Witness human excellence	Aspire to excellenc e	Gain skill and morality
Awe	Overwhelm ed by greatness	Accumula te he new	Safe as ap art of the larger whole

Love	Positive emotions in connection	Play, explore, savour, dream	Trust, bonds,community

Negativity bias is always present in us which is given to us through thousands of years of human evolution.

The negative emotions coexist with the positive emotions and on the whole we experience a little positive emotion during the day.

Broaden and Build Theory:

Each positive emotion urges us to take certain actions. Positive emotions prepare you for the future and negative emotions call for reactions at the moment. With positive emotions we become more resourceful and become more connected.

Positive emotions are like tiny engines, they drive growth.

Broadened awareness:

"There is a way of breathing that is a shame and suffocation. And there's another way of expiring a love-breath that lets you open infinitely."-Rumi, the thirteenth century poet.

Positivity is essential for human life in order for us to flourish just as plants require nutrients for their growth.

Positive emotions expand possibilities for people and expand our awareness.

People see the big picture when they experience positive emotions.

Built Resources:

"The days that make us happy, make us wise."-from John Masefield's poem, Biography

People's passions matter in a person's development.
The passion has a Domino Effect:

- Subtle increase in positive emotions
- Increases in resources in people's lives.
- Increased satisfaction with life.
- Reduced depressive symptoms.

Resilience:

We can experience positive emotions while experiencing difficult situations.

Resilience is about worrying less; rebounding quickly from a depressed state; being in the moment.

Resilient people recognize positive aspects with the negative aspects in a situation.

In difficult situations they think that it will pass. Positive emotions undo negativity.

Positive emotions and Entrepreneurship:
Entrepreneurship consists of facing the challenge of battles and failures. The entrepreneur essentially identifies the opportunity; builds the team to delivers the goods and services(must have an optimistic spirit); and gathering the resources to be deliver the goods or the services.

Measuring our positivity scores:
During the past twenty four hours of any given day we might have faced both positive and negative emotions. We can take the test at the website: www. Positiveratios.com. The website asks to self-evaluate your emotions during the past 24 hours by answering a

set of questions and we can determine our positivity and negativity scores. Then we calculate the P/N ratios.

Your condition	P/N Ratio
Pathology	1
Languishing	2 to 1
Flourishing	3 to 1

What is Love?

We all experience love feelings towards our spouse, parents, children , friends and pets. What exactly is love?

According to recent research, Love is not:

- Sexual desire
- Romance
- Commitment
- Bond
- Exclusive
- Unconditional
- Lasting

    A definition of love is as under:

    " Investment in the well-being of the other for his or her own sake."-Hegi & Bergner(2010)

    Emotions rise in us and then it fades away.

    Thus love can now be defined as:

    Love is

    - An interpersonally situated experience marked by momentary increases in

        -Shared positive emotions

        -Bio-behavioural synchrony

-Mutual care
- Which over time, builds:
-embodied rapport
-social bonds
Commitment.

a. Positivity resonance

When we meet another person with who we connect well we give a smile. When we see the other person in the eye, we can truly understand the meaning of that smile. There are fifty different kinds of smiles expressing different emotions. In telephonic conversations , the voice can express emotions. When two persons connect with each other, then oxytocin is generated in the brain. What is a smile for:

- To express positivity
- To evoke positivity
- To evoke inter-subjectivity
- To broaden collective mindsets and build collective resources.
- All of the above.
  When we experience positivity resonance we get life-giving nutrient for our well being.

b. Loving-Kindness Meditation

Bu this meditation w can become other-focused. By this method we spend some time with ourselves. This can bring positivity into our lives.

In this one repeats to oneself such phrases like the following for another person:

- May you feel safe

- May feel happy
- May you healthy
- May you live with ease.
  c. Cardiovascular benefits of positivity

When we are in sync with someone, it is energizing and life-affirming.

Vagus nerve connects brain with the heart. Vagus nerve helps you to calm down after a fright.

Cardiac vagal Tone predicts the body's ability to regulate:

- Heart rhythms
- Glucose
- Inflammation'

Cardiac Vagal Tone predicts the mind's ability to regulate:

- Attention
- Emotions
- Social skills
  Cardiac Vagal Tone is influenced by shared positivity.

  d. Immune benefits of positivity

Positive emotions and experiencing positive micro-moments boost our immune system.

  e. Savouring Our Connections:

At the end of the day before going to sleep think over three encounters during the day when you were positively connected with another human being. How close you felt to the other person and how much you were tune with the other person could be your thinking point.

f.   Gratitude

When someone does an act of kindness or thoughtfulness to you and you express how much that meant to you to your benefactor, then research has shown that the bond between you and the benefactor has strengthened. Every one's emotions are contagious. So we have to be careful about what emotions we display in public.

23. Happiness

Introduction

The subject of happiness has been considered by philosophers and thinkers over the ages. Many prescriptions have been made. There has been scientific research on the subject in the recent decades. This book tries to summarise the latest research findings and it is hoped the research will help us to achieve greater happiness in our lives.

What is Happiness?

a.   Philosophical view

Various philosophers have dwelt upon this subject. Their views on the subject are as under:

Confucius about 2500 years ago had said in The Analects , "….brigs the good things of others to completion and does not bring the bad things of others to completion."

As per Buddhism," If you want others to be ahppy, practice compassion; if you want to be happy practice compassion."

b.   Economic view

Economists view happiness as our well being.

c.   Scientific view

Happiness does not mean:

- To have all your personal needs met.
- Always feeling satisfied with life.
- Feeling pleasure all the time.
- Never feeling negative emotions.
- There is no uniform prescription for happiness—one size does not fit all.

How can be happy?

a. Friends

Friends are great sources of mental support. Friendless people are likely to die early and have heart problems.

b. Romantic partners

Romantic partners give us immense pleasure and also they can cause immense mental distress.

A relationship become sour when:

a. There is hatred towards each other.
b. When both partners respect and value each other.
c. When stone-walling occurs between the two. That is one party is prepared to veen not hear the other partner.

Is continuous happiness possible?

As per philosophical view, happiness and unhappiness rotate like the wheel. And nature does not want to see us happy all the time. One cannot be happy for a very long time. Sadness will eventually creep into one's life.

Perhaps happiness is a way of looking at the situation; looking at the brighter side of the situation, for half-full glass can be interpreted as either half full or half-empty. It is our thoughts which make us happy or unhappy. How we think about a situation makes us happy or unhappy.'

What makes us happy?

a. We think that good events will make us happy if they happen and it refers to the future. Like getting boy friend, having a baby or getting that fancy new car.

b. Heart brewaking events make us sad and with time recover and again become happy.

c. What gives us happiness: material possessions or experience. Some would argue that experience lingers with us and in our solitary moments the very thoughts of those experience makes us happy.

d. Money: Money by itself cannot give happiness. What we do with this money gives us things and experiences which may make us happy..

e. Spending on oneself versus spending on others: Recent research has shown if we spend time and money on others it will make us more happy compared to if we spent on ourselves.

f.

Why we become unhappy?

We become unhappy because things and events don't happen as we wish. People don't behave in the way we expect. Expectations when unfulfilled makes us sad.

Health Benefits of Happiness

Recent research has indicated the following health benefits of being happy.

    a. Happiness protects your heart.
    b. Happiness strengthens your immune system. That is you become resistant to infections and diseases.
    c. Happiness combats stress.
    d. Happy people have fewer aches and pains.
    e. Happiness combats disability.
    f. Happiness lengthens our lives.

A blueprint for happiness

It would seem that we connect positively with our surroundings.

We may feel micro moments of joy with a positive attitude towards life and fellow human beings. It is better o spend our money on others rather than ourselves.

If we want to be happy in our social relationships, we need to know what other people expect from us and try to meet their expectations.

We may practice mindfulness and see what thoughts arise in our mind and just watch them without praising or blaming them. Meditation , sitting in a quiet place, and just watching our thoughts and gradually become thoughtless will give us some mental peace.

24. Psychology of popularity

What is popularity?

Popularity can be seen with respect to each stage of a man's life.

Childhood: Normally we see that by the age three we come to know whether a child is popular or not.

Adolescents: There is pubertal brain changes in everyone. In this stage the person is oriented towards peers.

Adults: In this stage one is nostalgic. We can judge a person's popularity by the number of followers on the social media sites such as Facebook or Twitter.

Workplace: In this situation we ask questions such as:

a. Who is well-liked?
b. Who is most powerful/influential?
c. Who is most likely to be promoted.
   In social relations we can judge popularity by the following criteria:
   - The ability to make friends.
   - Dominance within the group of friends
   - Meeting romantic partners.

Does our DNA control our responses to popularity

Evolution favoured that we live in groups. Living in a herd was preferable for food, safety, and coordinated activities. Leaving the herd meant incurring more risk. Our brain signals when we may beat risk.

Our DNA is responsive to injury. Cells in our body regenerate. New cells grow based on DNA. Dormant cells are turned on by social experiences.

We have dispositions uniquely oriented towards popularity. In social interactions, we process the cues to determine our response.

Social Information processing takes place as under:

Event → Cue encoding →Cue interpretation→ Goal clarification→ Response construction→ Response decision→ Response enactment

Social Information biases

We all have biases:

a. Hostile attribution bias in children:
   Kids who are rejected by their peers see hostile attribution bias. In this bias the following pattern emerges in social information processing:
   Cue encoding: Encode hostile cues
   Cue attribution: attribute hostile intent
b. Rejection sensitivity bias

Popularity in Kids

Popularity in kids has been studying the behavior of kids in playgroups. It is observed kids fall into the following categories when they play:

a. Cooperative play
b. Isolated/solitary play
c. Rough & Tumble play
d. Parallel play- some what aloof from the group
   Another way to gauge popularity is to provide a list of their peers and ask them the circle who are the most liked and another list where they mark who is the least liked.

By calculating the number of votes on gets as most liked(LM) or least liked (LL) we can calculate their standardizes LM or LL scores. Social preference is determined by the difference between their LM and LL scores. Social impact is measured by adding up these two scores.

If we plot the LL and LM scores in two axes, We get the following five categories of popularity and the percentage of people who fall into such categories is indicated below:
1. Popular:15-20%
2. Rejected:15-20%
3. Neglected:15-20%
4. Controversial :5%
5. Average:35-50%

1. Popularity in adolescents
   In adolescents the term popular is more relevant than liked as a person may not be liked that much but still be popular like a celebrity status.
   In their case social reputation is measured. Members of a group are asked to rate all others about who are the most popular. And then the scores of each is computed.
2. Does the context changes our popularity?

   It is observed through research that our popularity almost remains constant in the long run even if the context of our existence changes.

3. Popularity in Adults/Work setting

In work settings popularity is dependent upon

- Who speaks first
- Whose comments move the group discussion forward
- Who understand the social norm
- who is aggressive

In relationships popularity is dependent upon

- are you always initiating contact?
- Are you interested in what the group wants, or just what you want?

4. Factors affecting popularity:

Popularity may be judged on two considerations: Likeability and dominance/status. The factors which affect popularity may be as under:

- Behaviours
- Physical appearance
- Intelligence
- Family factors

a. Kids

It is observed that kids with different levels of popularity such as popular, neglected, rejected etc when put in a new setting tend to reach their original levels of popularity. This is dependent on how much did they initiate play with others and how much time did they spend playing with them.

Rejected kids were generally aggressive and did not read their environment well.

The popularity amongst kids is dependent upon their sociability and aggressive behavior .Some other factors are:

- Athletic ability
- Cooperativeness
- Leadership
- Friendship skills
- Positive social interactions

Rejected kids were those who were

- Easily angered
- Physically aggressive
- Unhappy
- Tense
- Anxious

Controversial kids were

- Funny
- Make kids laugh.

b. Facial attractiveness: If one is facially attractive one tends to be popular. Controversial persons are generally more physically attractive. Even infants show preference for attractive faces. Attractive people have many opportunities for social interaction and they have more wealth and more access to mate selection. Symmetry suggests health and such couples may produce healthy offsprings. Parents also treat children differently depending upon their attractiveness. Very lean or vey obese

people have less social reputation. But now fewer and fewer people have idealized shapes anymore.
   c. Variation in popularity from childhood to adulthood:
5. Different forms of aggression:
It can be in either of the two forms:
Overt/physical
Relational
Overt/physical:
- Hits/shoves or pushes others
- Threatens others
- Calls names, teases

Relational:

This can be seen in two different types:

Damage a relationship.

- Ignores others
- Gives peers the silent treatment
- Excludes others from activities
- Threatens to stop being a friend

Damage a social reputation:

- Spread rumours/gossip
- Tries to get peers to stop liking someone
- Says mean things behind one's back
  Research has shown boys normally engage in overt aggression and girls and boys both engage in relational aggression.
  Functions of aggression:

- reactive aggression
- Proactive aggression

Frustration aggression hypothesis:

Aggression is shown as a response to frustration.

Response to frustration:

- Internally derived
- Externally derived
- Uncontrolled, hot-blooded

Proactive aggression:

- This is normally goal directed

6. Health Risk Behaviours

   Health risk behaviours consists of substance use, sexual risk behaviours, self injurious behaviours and weight-related behaviours.

   The following are the findings of some research studies:

   a. Adolescents who use substances also engage in alcohol and marijuana consumption.
   b. Those who substances have a greater chance of having cardiovascular and cancer in adult period.

7. Sexual Risk behaviours

   Mitted diseases are Over 1 million teenage pregnancies occur in the US>Three million sexually transmitted infections are noticed in teens.

   Rate of HIV infection is growing fastest in adolescents and young adults.

Early engagement in sexual intercourse predicts lower use of STI protection and higher incidence of cervical cancer in adulthood.

25. Concepts and Theories of   Psychology

1. Anger Management

Anger is just one alphabet away from danger. A good manager should never be angry or lose his temper under any circumstance at the work-place. Anger is appropriately called brief madness. When we are angry we do or say things that we regret later. Successful anger management consists of :

1. To recognize signs that occur in your body when you become angry.
2. Take action to calm down.
3. Deal with the situation in a positive way.
   Coping with anger is learned behavior. You need anger management :
   1. When you indulge in physical violence.
   2. When you make threats of violence against people and property.
   3. When you indulge in out-of-control behaviour such as breaking things or driving recklessly.

Steps in anger management consist of:

1. Identify stressors which give rise to anger: frustration, financial stress, issues with a co-worker.

2. Pay attention to physical signs which arise in your body when angry.

3. Calm yourself.

4. Express feelings and needs assertively but not aggressively.

5. Focus on problem solving rather than blaming people.

2. Depression
   It is a state of mind producing serious, long-term lowering of enjoyment of life or inability to visualize a happy future. It is a period of unhappiness or low morale which lasts longer than several weeks and may include ideation of self-inflicted injury or suicide.
3. Motivation

   Motivation is that condition at workplace which propels employees to give their best and make efforts to achieve the assigned goals. Motivation of employees is dependent on
   1. Quality of supervision.
   2. Salary benefits.
   3. Relationship with peers.
   4. Prevalence of equity at the workplace.
   5. Challenging work.
   6. Scope for advancement and growth at the job.
   7. Company leadership at every level is responsible for motivating the employees.
   8. Employees should be respected.
   9. Leaders should assume the role of a coach.
   10. Create learning opportunities for employees.

11. Have an honest and open communication environment.
12. Give employees opportunity to fail and try again.
13. People should enjoy work.
14. The working environment should challenge individuals and teams to achieve significant goals.
15. The mangers should be friendly and approachable.
16. The manager must motivate himself first.
17. The manager must know his employees.
18. Don't reprimand your subordinates in the public.
19. Plan, don't procrastinate.
20. Get back if you fall.
21. Write down what you want to do.
22. Take calculated risks rather than harsh actions.

We are motivated to do things we find meaningful. Doing the same task over and over without a sense of purpose can be de-motivating. Appreciating people's work make them feel good about their work and thus motivates them. On the other hand ignoring people can be very de-motivating.

4. Attribution: When we succeed , we attribute the causes to ourselves and when we fail we attribute to outside causes.
5. Herzberg's Hygiene theory of Motivation

Certain factors , like challenging job, at the workplace motivate and cause job satisfaction and certain other separate factors(hygiene factors) cause dissatisfaction.

6. Abraham Maslow's Hierarchy of Needs

    Psychologist Abraham Maslow has identified five levels of needs for human beings. Every employee is at a particular level of need satisfaction. They are:

    1. Physiological: Such as breathing, food, water, sex, sleep and excretion.
    2. Safety: Security of body, employment, resources, morality, the family, health and property.
    3. Love/belonging needs: Friendship, family, sexual intimacy.
    4. Esteem needs: Self-esteem, confidence, achievement, respect of others, and respect by others.
    5. Self-actualisation needs: Morality, creativity, spontaneity, problem-solving, lack of prejudice and acceptance of facts.

    In an ideal organization it would be possible to satisfy their self-actualisation needs. In this state the employee will be highly productive, creative and innovative contributing to the growth of the organization.

7. Cognitive Dissonance

    First propounded by Leon Festinger , it is the tension that results when there is a mismatch between our beliefs and behavior. Sometimes employees may be in such a situation which causes stress and should be avoided. Dissonance   influences decisions. Dissonance may also follow a choice which has already been don

8. Communication

Managers spend 50 to 80 per cent of their time in communicating. Communication can be verbal or non-verbal. In verbal communication tone of the speaker is more important than the text. In non-verbal communication body language and eye contact show the sincerity of the communicator. For communication to be effective a climate of trust and openness should be created in the organization.

9. Non-Verbal Communication

It is the process of communication through sending and receiving wordless(mostly visual) cues between people. This involves voice, touch, distance and the use of time. It also involves eye contact while talking and listening, frequency of glances, pupil dilation and blink rate. Speech also involves elements such as voice quality, rate, pitch, volume and speaking style. One has to be conscious of elements non-verbal communication while interacting with other people.

10. Conversations

Here are some principles of a meaningful conversation.

   a.   Be brief
   b.   Be orderly.
   c.   Avoid obscurity
   d.   Avoid ambiguity.
   e.   Be relevant.
   f.   Don't say what you don't believe.

11. Dealing with failures & Criticism

    Past failures should not hold you back. There are no failures but experiences. One should learn from the failures. Failure is the fertilizer for success. Criticisms should not be taken personally. It should be examined if they are fair; then one should make efforts to overcome the negative trait. Or else they should be ignored. Soichiro Honda had said, "Success is ninety-nine percent failure and one per cent what you learn from these failures."

12. Halo effect: It is the phenomenon where we evaluate somebody globally and then apply it to their specific traits. For example we might think somebody likeable. Because of this , we might assume that they are intelligent, friendly and display good judgment.

13. Emotional Intelligence: It is the ability to identify , assess and control the emotions of oneself, of others and of groups.

    Relationship with the boss and sub-ordinates
    The relationship with the boss should one of respect and inspiring confidence. The subordinate should be trustworthy and should not never quarrel with the boss. The boss may differ from one's views on the basis of his experience. The subordinate should state his views honestly and if the boss doesn't agree with them, then he should toe the boss's line provided it is not illegal or against company policy.

14. Extrovert: This concept was first popularized by Carl Jung. These types of persons are considered to be a

particular type where the person is outgoing, talkative and shows energetic behavior.

15. First Impressions

Often one needs to create good first impression for the following reasons:

A. One's relationship with a person and in some cases, one's career depends upon what the other person thinks of you upon your first meeting.

B. Bad impressions are often difficult to undo.

C. For sales people first impressions may make or break a deal.

What can we do make a first impression?:

1. Dress for success and to project confidence.

2. You should look professional and well-groomed.

3. Try to appear confident.

4. Establish rapport with a smile, hand shake and body language.

5. The handshake should be firm and make eye to eye contact.

6. Don't hurry your conversation.

16. Introvert: These are peoole who are more reserved and solitary in nature.

17. Johari Window

It is what we know about ourselves and what others think they know about us.

It is made up of four quadrants:

1. Open self: What others know about us and we know too.

2. Blind self: What others know about you, but you don't.

3.   Hidden self: What others do not know about you, but youy do. It is your secrets.
4.   Unknown self: What others don't know about you and you don't either.

18. Just World Hypothesis: According to this hypothesis whatever happens is just. People become victims since they deserved it.

19. Leadership

Is leadership an in-born trait or can it be learned? Although some people tend to be born leaders , others can understand the underlying tenets and try to become a better leader. Chinese Book of Wisdom (660 B.C.) gives us insight to the idea of leadership thus," Most leadership are despised, some leaders are feared, few leaders are praised, and the rare good leader is never noticed."It can be said to be the art of inducing obedience, as a way of convincing people of exercising influence and as an instrument for achieving goals. All leadership is influence. Leaders have to confront head on the major problems of society or an organization. Control is not leadership. Management is not leadership. Leadership is leadership. We will see later the qualities required of a leader and how he should deal with his peers and followers. Leadership is not a formula or a programme. It is an attitude. It comes from the heart and reaches out to the hearts of others. A true leader endeavors to serve the people he leads. Leadership is the art of getting someone else to do something you want done because he wants to do it. Leadership is based on goodwill. It means obvious and wholehearted commitment to helping the followers. Great leaders gain authority by giving it away Leadership is not magnetic personality. It is not making friends and influencing people. It is lifting a person's vision to higher heights. Leadership is about inspiration –of oneself and of others. Leadership is not status quo. It is trying to shape a better future. Leaders make their followers self-motivated to achieve the goals set. Leadership is facing the challenges. Leaders help other people. Leaders' character should inspire confidence. Leadership is to be able to rally men for a common purpose. Leaders inspire people to make a difference. Leadership is not formula or a routine. It comes from the heart and reaches out to the hearts of others. Leadership and learning are indispensable to each other. It cannot be taught but must be learned. Leadership is not being popular but doing what is right. Leadership is a healthy disregard of the impossible. It is about creating the right emotions in people and ensuring that these emotions help the individual. Leadership means trying new things.

LEADERSHIP AND THE PERSONAL QUALITIES OF A LEADER

Leadership is creating an environment where you can invite the best and the brightest people to your company while exercising judgment and autonomy and share glory of the company along with your employees over and above financial rewards.

2.1. A leader makes himself loved without courting love.
2.2 A leader should be able to define reality.
2.3 A leader has the ability to do things differently.
2.4 A leader has knowledge and ability to execute his ideas.
2.5 A leader should be large hearted.
2.6 Leader should do innovation for growth.
2.7 A leader should have integrity. He should be the same on the inside and on the outside.
2.7 A leader should know what he wants and must be able to make it clear ot those around him.
2.8 A leader should be credible.
2.9 A leader has to concentrate on mid-term and long term goals.
2.10 A leader thinks from user's point of view.
2.11 A leader acts like a catalyst for change.
2.12 A leader works on the system while a manager works in it.
2.13 A real leader has no need to lead but points the way.
2.14 Leaders have clear vision.
2.15 Leaders act as role models.
2.16 Leaders spend time on tasks which they really enjoy.

1.   Leaders in Action

1.1 The leader asks "what" and why" whereas the manager asks "how" and "when".

1.2 A leader facilitates the work of those who work for him.

1.3 The leader brings out the best amongst his followers.

1.4 Leadership is basically a relationship which is established through interactions.

1.5 Leaders inspire through hope and vision.

1.6 Leaders spread compassion

1.7 Leaders are mindful: attuned to the mind, body, heart and spirit of his followers.

1.8 A leader inspires others by creating and maintaining resonance with his followers.

1.9 A leader focuses on nurturing and developing leaders from amongst his followers.

1.10

The leader says "let's go" while a boss says " go".

1.11

The leader takes less credit for success and gives credit for success to the team and owns up the failures of his team.

1.12

The leader concentrates on his personal growth.

1.13

The leader acts with speed.

1.14

The leader undertakes to do more than he can do and finally does it.

1.15

The leader carries his people with a clear vision.

1.16

The leader deals with his people directly and has no hidden agenda.

1.17

The leader delegates his responsibilities but reviews the performance and gives feedback.

1.18

The leader develops his people.

1.19

The leader displays openness and curiosity and learns from anyone , anywhere.

1.20

leader motivates his people to confront challenges.

1.21

The leader focuses on finding solutions and achieving results rather than making excuses and shifting blame for nonperformance.

1.22

The leader emphasizes we rather than I.

1.23

The leader generates ideas.

1.24

The leader has vision and works like an entrepreneur.

1.25

The leader has common sense and a sense of humour to tide over awkward situations.

1.26

The leader has conviction and courage.

1.27

The leader has to be optimistic and zealous.

1.28

The leader leads by example.

1.29

The leader understand the strengths, aspirations and patterns of behavior of his people.

1.30

The leader helps people to be their best by providing coaching and feedback.

1.31

The leader is a creative person and invents the future.

1.32

The leader is dedicated to his goals.

1.33

The leader is ever curious.

1.34

The leader is humble.

1.35

The leader has hunger to learn.

1.36

The leader is excellent in execution.

1.37

The leader is one who knows the way, goes the way and shows the way.

1.38

The leader keeps his promises and understands that business is about relationships. If people like you they buy from you.

1.39

The leader is capable.

1.40

The leader must be dedicated. He should spend the time and energy to accomplish the tasks at hand.

1.41

The leader should be open-minded and should be open to new ideas.

1.42

The leader knows his people, their strengths and weaknesses.

1.43

The leader takes quick decision with the incomplete set of information available.

1.44

The leader never underestimates competition.

1.45

The leader produces ideas.

1.46

The leader promotes a positive energizing, optimistic and fun environment.

1.47

The leader promotes and implements innovative and creative ideas and solutions.

1.48

The leader questions existing ways and finds new ways.

1.49

The leader recognises a problem before it becomes an emergency.

1.50

The leader remains dissatisfied with the current status.

1.51

The leader says "Thank you" and "please" more.

1.52

The leader sets aside assumptions, reverses roles and learns from every person in the organization.

1.53

The leader accepts responsibility.

1.54

The leader should be able to deliver results continually.

1.55

The leader has clarity about the goals he pursues.

1.56

The leader should be magnanimous and

ensures that credit for success is given to as many people as possible throughout the organization.

1.57

The leader should be passionate, positive and polite.

1.58

The leader should do straight talk.

1.59

The leader should have an analytical mind.

1.60

The leader solicits and gives honest feedback.

1.61

The leader tries something different.

1.62

The leader tries to be the best in the world in his field.

1.63

The leader tries to be competent.

1.64

The leader tries be to highly credible.

1.65

The leader tries to build enduring relationships with the customers.

1.66

The leader tries to give a better product and a better services to its customers.

1.67

The leader tries to identify the inhibitors to tem work and removes or overcomes them.

1.68

The leader ties to impress its customers.

1.69

The leader tries to make his people productive.

1.70

The leader tries to understand his business space, his competition and his targets.

1.71

The leader tries to understand why people behave the way they do.

1.72

The leader uses the people's ideas for improvement.

1.73

The leader wins the respect of employees, customers, stakeholders and investors.

1.74

The leader works for collaboration.

1.75

He respects each individual, listens and learns with them.

A leader works with others as a team to accomplish results and to win.

1.76

After failures, a leader rectifies errors and moves on.

1.77

The leader should be passionate to make his vision a reality.

1.78

The leader is strong, fit and fast.

1.79

The leader is a team builder.

1.80

The leader is disciplined at work.

1.81

The leader is humble about his success.

1.82

leader tries for his individual growth.

1.83

The leader is a perennial learner.

1.84

The leader empowers his subordinates and does not manage them.

1.85

The leader encourages his subordinates to express opinions and ideas.

1.86

The leader encourages integrity at the workplace.

1.87

The leader engages the people for building the future.

1.88

The leader shows average people that they can do the work of superior people.

1.89

A good leader is a simplifier.

1.90

 The good leader supports the bottom ten percent.

1.91

 The leader uses his power but lightly.

1.92

 The leader should be prepared to give blood, toil, tears and sweat.

1.93

 The leader does whatever he asks others to do.

1.94

 The leader keeps his friends close and his enemies closer.

1.95

 The leader leads from the back and lets his followers take the credit.

1.96

 Leaders cultivate respect by giving it.

1.97

 The leader is truthful and trustworthy.

1.98

 I The eader states his expectations clearly and tries to remove any misunderstanding.

1.99

 Leaders adapt to actual situations.

1.100

 Leaders aim for continuous improvement.

1.101

 Leaders are assertive but not aggressive.

1.102

Leaders are fair and they deal with others consistently and justly.

1.103

Leaders are good at networking and help others to achieve their goals.

1.104

A leader tries to connect with people who work for him.

1.105

A leader coaches his team and organization for success.

1.106

A leader tries to create a creative work environment.

1.107

Leaders create conditions so that employees love their job and give their best performance.

1.108

A leader deals with his employees with dignity and respect.

1.109

Leaders don't nit-pick, constantly criticize over small things, belittle, judge, de-mean or patronize. They are impartial.

1.110

Leaders dream fearlessly.

1.111

Leaders find corruption, fight it and destroy it.

1.112

A leader focuses on the future.

1.113

A leader focuses on what he could do.

1.114

Leaders give opportunities to their people.

1.115

Leaders go first. They do not wait. They take the lead and initiate.

1.116

Leaders groom their people for bigger roles.

1.117

Leaders have the power to inspire other people.

1.118

Leaders inspect the work of their juniors and give comments and suggestions.

1.119

Leaders encourage their people to tak risks.

1.120

Leaders lead by example.

1.121

Leaders listen to what others have to say before expressing their viewpoint. They never cut off people.

1.122

Leaders look at the bigger picture.

1.123

Leaders seek new solutions to old problems.

1.124

Leaders seek responsibility and volunteer.

1.125

A leader should feel the ownership of the organization he elads.

1.126

Leaders study the market.

1.127

Leaders take chances and grab the opportunities.

1.128

Leaders try to bring out the best in others.

1.129

Leaders try to give back to the world.

1.130

Leaders try to put ideas into practice.

1.131

Leaders work from the heart.

1.132

Leaders work on the system.

1.133

Leaders try to shape the future.

1.134

Leaders do not shy away from challenges.

1.135

If you use an employee's idea then let them know it or better encourage the person with the idea to implement the idea.

1.136

Leaders do not give orders which cannot be obeyed.

1.137

A leader optimises the cost and reduces unnecessary cost.

1.138

A leader tries to boost the self-esteem of the persons he leads.

1.139

A leader leads whereas a boss drives.

1.140

A leader does not intimidate his people.

1.141

A leader does not hit people on the head.

1.142

A leader does not humiliate people.

1.143

A leader should inspire others to dream more, learn more, do more and become more.

1.144

A leader should be able to inspire others to dream more, learn more, do more and become more.

1.145

True leaders are humble.

1.146

A leader never stops learning.

1.147

Leaders should ask the right questions instead of looking at the right answers.

1.148

Leaders set 3 to 5 key priorities.

1.149

L:eaders believe in teamwork.

1.150

Leadership is about making others better as

a result of our presence and making sure that impact lasts in your absence.

Some of principles of leadership are stated below:

a. Leader's behavior affects the satisfaction of the group members and group performance.

b. When competence of subordinates is ensured, a participative leadership will result in better decisions.

c. A good leader should be sensitive to the needs of the group members in varying situations.

d. There can be various forms of leadership such as autocratic where the leader makes the decision without making inquiries with the group. Or the leader makes the decision after making selective enquiries.

e. Consultative leaders make the decision after he has asked individual members of the group for solutions. Or the leader makes the decision after consulting and discussing with the whole group.

f. In democratic leadership the group including the leader makes the decision.

It would seem the type of leadership will depend upon the situation. Before deciding which type of leadership to adopt the leader may ask the following questions:

a. Do I have sufficient information to make a high quality decision/

b. Is acceptance of the decision making by subordinates is critical to effective implementation
c. If I were to make the decision myself, is it reasonably certain that I would be accepted by my subordinates?
d. Is conflict among subordinates likely in the preferred solution?

14. Life Position

Our attitude to life depends upon our life positions.

****

15. Depression

It is considered present when suicidal thoughts exists for more than 2 weeks. When it feels that life is useless. It can be treated with medicines. I t is reduced by indulging in physical activity.

15. Mental Illness

Abnormal behavior or mental illness is a an increasingly important public health issue. It is the most common form of human disease. One in five of all mankind is likely to suffer from this ailment.

Behaviour thus can be deviant, abnormal or maladaptive. Societal norms may decide what behavior is normal and what is not. Abnormal behavior is determined by the guidelines laid down in the DSM(Diagnostic and Stastical Manual of Mental Disorders.

16. Devil's Advocate

In meetings and discussions in order to improve the decision quality, one person amongst the group takes up the role of a devil's advocate who takes the position of the dversary or the other party and puts up views of the other party which the group might have ignored.

17. John Stacey Adam's Equity Theory
According to this theory employees seek to maintain equity between the inputs they bring to a job and the outcomes they receive from it against the perceived inputs and outputs of thers. So to get the best from the employees there should be no partiality anf rewrads should be commensurate with the efforts put in by the employees.

Effort1/Reward1 =Effort2/Reward2

20. Stress Management

We experience stress when
a. Our expectations are not met.
b. When the reality around you changes and
c. Unexpected events occurring in your life and we cannot cope with the pressure.

We can neutralise stress by trying to change the reality which may create more stress. We feel stress when we do not get what we want. We can manage stress by:

a. Pause for 2 -3 seconds before responding to any event.
b. Adopt a detached perspective towards yourself and the event by overcoming your ego.
c. Try to observe your mind and ego.
d. Try to have silent moments in between working hours.
e. If possible meditate for one minute every one hour.
f. Eat a healthy diet.
g. Get regular exercises.
h. Get plenty of sleep.
i. Have a sense of humour.

21. Working in Groups

Bruce Tuckman's Group Development Model

In an organisation it is essential sometimes to form groups to achieve organizational goals. There are some obstacles to effective group performance. Bruce Tuckman has suggested the following model to enable us to understand their fiunctioning and steps we can take to make them effective.

    a. Forming stage: In this stage group memeebers learn to know each other. There is a need for the team leader to control the group at this atge.

    b. Storming stage: Group members come to know the divergetnn views of the members.

    c. Norming stage: Memebrs agree for a common goal. There is collaboration and constructive criticism.

    d. Performing stage: There is no conflict in the group and the group is productive.

    e. Adjourning stage: Now the project is completed.

22. Conflict Management

Conflicts do occur at the workplace. The sources of conflicts are:

a. People disagree: They see things differently because of differences in understanding and viewpoints and personality differences. Half-full glass of one person can be half-empty of another.

b. People have different styles, principles, values, beliefs and slogans which determine their choices and objectives. A risk-taking manager would be in conflict with a risk-minimising manager who believes in firm control and a well-kept routine.

e. People have different thinking styles.

f. people are concerned with fear, force, fairness or funds.

1. Ambiguous jurisdiction: two individuals have responsibilities which are inter-dependent.
2. Conflict of interest.
3. Communication barrier.
4. Dependence on one party by another group or individual.
5. Unresolved prior conflicts.
   Conflict situations should be resolved and used beneficially. It can have both positive and negative effects.
   Positive effects:
   1. Diffusion of more serious conflicts.
   2. Stimulation of a search for new facts or resolutions.
   3. Increase in group cohesion and performance.

4. Assessment f power.

Negative Effects:

1. They create obstacles to smooth working.
2. Diminishing output.
3. Obstructions in the decision making process.
4. Formation of competing affiliations in the organization.
5. Conflict reduces employees' commitment to organizational goals and organizational efficiency.

   Thus conflicts may be unavoidable. It is better to match power, organizational demands and self-esteem. Various ideas and viewpoints can be subsumed into innovation. Better ideas and methods can be developed. Conflict can be motivator for healthy change. In order to manage conflicts better an organizations needs to

   a. Improve policies, procedures and rules.
   b. Move people across functions so that get a broader viewpoint,
   c. Minimize authority or domain related issues
   d. Ask what and why rather than who, to get to the roots of a problem.

23. Social Psychology
It is the scientific study of how people's thoughts, feelings and behaviours are influenced by the actual, perceived or implied presence of others.
24. De-individuation
   The concept was enunciated by Leon Festinger. It occurs when individuals are not

seen or paid attention to as individuals. The members don't feel that they stand out as individuals(and there is) a reduction of inner restraints against doing various things.

24. Decision Making
It is better to consult the employees while deciding on matters related to them. Two heads are always better than one. People working on the ground know the best. A manager should not impose his decisions on his employees by force. They should be accepted to his sub-ordinates. The manager may not have all information with him to take a right decision. While deciding ,alternatives should be considered and the course of action which yields optimum results should be taken. For this brain storming with the concerned people in group of ten to twelve people should be carried out. In brain-storming the ideas may be welcomed and all ideas may be noted down. People should not be snubbed for giving seemingly impractical or useless ideas. Other factors to be taken into considerations are;
   1. Are decisions opinion driven or data driven.
   2. Are decisions driven by vision?
   3. Is the right question is being asked?
   4. How much data is required for knowledge or insight?
   5. What are the potential outcomes?
   6. What is right acceptable level f risk?
   7. Does he range of options affect outcomes?
   8. Are we measuring the right factors?

9. How long is our decision loop?

25. Giving feedback to Sub-ordinates
It is a good idea that a manager gives feedback on the performance to his sub-ordinates. Many managers keep their juniors in suspense which prevents performance improvement if any deficiency exists. But giving feedback in a blunt manner can be traumatic. Thus the purpose of giving feedback to your juniors is to give them a chance to develop. Try to be factual rather than judgmental. It is a good idea to adopt the sandwich method. In this method the manager first praises the person and the criticism is given. Express issues and concerns rather than opinions. Don't leave on a negative note. At last leave on a positive note.

26. Managing People
The achievements of an organization are the results of the combine effort of each individual. Human resources are the most important factor in the success of the organization. For they can be creative and innovative to face the challenges of competition and give customer delight to their customers so the business or the organization can survive and grow. Yet human resources are the most complex and difficult to manage as they are unique, have individual difference and are members of groups. Some basic principles are as under:

    a. Employees should not be criticized or humiliated in public but should be reprimanded in private.

b. The tone of communication with the employees is as important as the content of communication.

c. They should be praised for the good work they do and their bad behavior should be ignored for some time.

d. All punishments need not be punitive.

e. It is the duty of the manager to keep the employees happy.

f. The manager must understand the aspirations of his employees.

g. The manager must offer challenging careers to its employees.

A business makes money by adding value to its customers. Happy and highly engaged employees will result in happy customers which in turn will results in income or profits. How you treat your employees will make your employees happy and engaged. While strategic focus(planning and prioritization)and operational excellence(pace and processes) are necessary for growth, they are not sufficient. Growth of a business requires the right kind of people, culture and leadership. Growth requires the hiring, training and retaining of high performance employees and the building of a high performance management team. How a manager treats his employees will depend upon whether he believes in theory X or Y which was propounded by Douglas Mc Gregor.

A senior manager may have to manage many managers under him which is basically a teaching or coaching process. Every manager is a different person and one has to learn how that individual learns and responds to feedback etc.

Senior managers have to act like leaders. You cannot lead unless you have willing followers. Engaging followers takes time and emotional intelligence- a skill that many people lack.

Managers have to often delegate their authority. Delegation is a learned skill and it is a process.

27. Douglas McGregor theory X &Y
Theory X considers people to be a cost to be controlled and monitored.
Theory Y views people as an asset to be valued and developed.

28. Mentoring and Coaching
As senior managers one may have to build trusting and open relationship while holding people accountable for high performance. The role requires even more emotional intelligence and engagement and time to deal with personal issues and style.

29. Mediation
It is the role one takes to sort out the differences between two parties.

30. SELF-FULFILLING PROPHECIES

It was first propounded by Robert Merton in 1948. He stated, " The self-fulfilling prophecy, is, in the beginning, a false definition of the situation evoking a new behaviour which makes the originally false conception come true(thereby perpetuating) reign of error. For the prophet will cite actual course of events as proof of being right from the beginning. Such are the perversities of social logic" The theory has been experimented in school, college and job setting. Rosenthal conducted this study in schools and name it as Pygmalion effect after the play of George Bernard Shaw which depicted a flower girl being taught to speak and learn by a professor actually came up-to the expectations. As a corollary of this theory, we observe behavioural confirmation.

Behavioural confirmation: It takes place when people's social expectations lead them to act in a way that causes others to confirm these expectations. It's is a social type of self-fulfilling prophecy.

31. Team functioning

   Teams may perform better than individuals. In this age of specialization it is better to pool human resources into a team to address organizational challenges.

TEAM may mean Together We Achieve More. A manager has to keep the following in mind to build his team.

   1. Lead by example: The manager should act a model of behavior and performance for his team members.

2. Discussing a core value of the team every day: Every day a few minutes of the staring period may be used in discussing the core values of the team which may reinforce them.

3. Coaching: Inspire other members of the team to do things which they thought they could never do. Grow more leaders in the team.

4. Share human moments: To build a cohesive team celebrate together. Have fun together. Get to know the family members of your employees and them as human beings.

32. Practical tips for Team Management

Members of a team should be chosen carefully. Right people should be put in position so that you don't have to shift their positions later.

Invest time and effort in creating the team that you would put in recruiting a new employee.

Make every member of the team special.

Teams should have the backing of the top management.

Teams should have free access to and sharing of information.

Truth should be told clearly and honestly.

Acknowledge and appreciate the contribution of others.

Consider every problem as a challenge in disguise.

33. Conformity: It I a change in behavior or belief as a result of social pressure.

34. Group dynamics: It refers to psychological processes and behaviours that occur either

- Within a group(intergroup dynamics)
- Between groups(intergroup dynamics)

35. Groupthink: It is a phenomenon in which decision making suffers when a cohesive group becomes insulated from dissenting viewpoints , especially when the group leader promotes a particular solution or course of action.

To avoid group think in discussions, debate should be welcomes. Japanese have found a way of allowing their lowest rank employees to speak first in meeting so that they do not have o contradict their superiors.

36. Abilene Paradox : It is the phenomenon when people in a group take an action in contradiction to their individual references to satisfy the members of the group. This happens due to :

1. Action anxiety

2. Negative fantasies prevent us from taking the desired action.

3. Real risk is often there.

4. Fear of separation from our loved ones.

5. Confusion of fantasy and reality.

6. Identifying whom to blame.

7. Blaming the leader.

This paradox can be avoided by : 1. Assess the real risks of taking or not taking action. 2. Speak up your feelings frankly.

3.Confront the group.

36. Perception

It is the organization, identification and interpretation of sensory information in order to represent and understand the environment.
Perception is achieved through signals in the nervous system which is ntitiated from physical or chemical stimulation of the sense organ. For example vision involves light striking the retina of the eye, smell driven by odour molecules.

37. Inference

It is the act or process of deriving logical conclusions from premises known or assumed to be true. Human inference is studied within the field of cognitive psychology.

38. Change blindness

It is the psychological phenomenon that occurs when a change in a visual stimulus goes unnoticed by the observer. For example an individual fails to notice a difference between two images that are identical except for one change.

39. Choice blindness

We really don't know the real reasons as to why we take a particular decision. When asked about the reasons for our decision we cannot always give the real reason.Often we agree for conflicting or opposite decisions and we cook a story for our reason.

40. Prejudices: We like to think in terms of categorical thinking such as male or female, white or   black etc.

41. Hindsight bias: If you are told of some conclusions or facts, you always guess it right.

42. 80/20 Rule: We achieve 80 percent of our results from 20 percent of our activities.

43. Halo effect: We evaluate somebody globally, but then apply it to their specific traits. For example, we might think somebody is likeable. Because they are likeable, we might assume they are intelligent, friendly and display good judgment.

44. Prisoner's Dilemma

In this dilemma, one analyses one's response/behavior in relation to expectations of others' behaviours. Such a dilemma results in sub-optimal outcomes.

45. TRANSACTIONAL ANALYSIS

Whenever two persons interact it can be observed that both of them behave from the following three ego-states. Inappropriate behaviour at the workplace can give rise to conflicts.

1.Parent: The person behaves in a manner such his parent would have responded to the situation.

2.Adult:The person behaves without emotion and makes an objective appraisal of reality.

3.Child:People behave feel, behave and think similarly to how they did in childhood. There is spontaneity and intimacy in the transaction. In an organizational setting it is better if everybody behaved in adult ego states.

46. INTER-PERSONAL RELATIONS

A relationship is the connection between two individuals. Sometimes these relationships create discomfort for us and make the work environment unpleasant. Here some thoughts which could be of use to managers.

1. If somebody indulges in a behaviour which causes us pain or unease, then forgive that person in order to forget the interaction.
2. When we interact with each other, focus on the good qualities of the other person rather than the bad qualities.
3. When we stop talking with another person the relationship becomes bitter. Due to ego one does not take the initiative to talk. In such situations one may take the initiative to start talking. By bending , we are not weak.
4. The subordinate should show loyalty to the boss and gain the latter's confidence.
5. Don't quarrel and become enemies at the workplace.
6. Boss's role is to facilitate the work of his subordinates.
7. People disagree as they see things differently because of differences in understanding and viewpoint.

8. People have different styles, principles, values and beliefs which determine their choices and objectives.

9. People have different ideological and philosophical outlooks.

10. What and why should be asked and not who to get to the roots of a problem.

47. ORANISATIONAL CULTURE

It is the shared rules governing cognitive and affective aspects of membership in an organization and the means whereby they are shaped and expressed. It can be used as a means to control normative behavior of employees.

48. Elements of Inspiring Leadership

In order that a leader inspires his subordinates to become their better selves and realize their potential , he must have the following qualities.

a. Emotional Intelligence:

1. Emotional Self-Awareness
2. Adaptability
3. Emotional self-control
4. Positive outlook
5. Achievement Orientation

b. Social Intelligence

1. Empath y

2. Teamw
ork
3. Networ
king
4. Develo
ping
others.

c. Cognitive Intelligence

1. S
y
s
t
e
m
s

t
h
i
n
k
i
n
g
2. P
a
t
t
e
r
n

recognition.

49. Managing Change

Change from the status-quo would require actions for affective change. This involves making a strategic plan. To make a strategic plan one has to think it mentally and then give it a physical manifestation.

Components of a strategic plan are:

1. Vision: Develop a clear vision.
2. Mission: Define what is this about at the core.
3. Values: Identify the most important values.
4. Strategy: Choose one to three strategic steps.

50. Requirements for creativity

The following obstacles are generally faced in achieving what we want to do:

1. Fear
2. Lack of focus.
3. We are afraid to make experiments.

51. Human Brain

he human brain is considered to have a left area and a right area which are responsible for different functions.

Broca's area: It is the region of the frontal lobe of one hemisphere(usually the left) brain with the functions linked to speech production. It is named after Pierre Paul Broca who discovered that patients had lost the ability to speak after injury to this area.

Wernicke's area: This area named after Carl Wernicke, one of the two parts of the cerebral cortex linked since the late 19th century to speeeech. It is involved in understanding of the written and spoken language. Destruction of Wernicke's area

Male brains are much more laterised than the female brains.

Brain stem: It is the posterior part of the brain, adjoining and structurally continuous with the spinal cord. Its functions are controlling heart rate, breathing, sleeping and eating.

Diseases of the brain stem can lead to visual disturbances, pupil abnormalities, changes in sensation, muscle weakness, hearing problems, vertigo, swallowing and speech difficulty, voice change and coordination problems.

52. Personality

It refers to the pattern of thoughts, feelings, social adjustments, and behaviours consistently exhibited over time that strongly influences one's expectations, self-perceptions, values and attitudes. It also predicts human reactions to other people, problems and stress.

Id, Ego and Super ego: Sigmund Freud divides human personality into three significant components: the id, ego and super-ego.

The id: It acts according to the pleasure principle, demanding immediate gratification of its needs regardless of external environment.

Ego: It realistically meets the wishes and demands of the id in accordance with the outside world, adhering to the reality principle.

Super-ego: (Conscience). It inculcates moral judgments and societal rules upon the go, thus forcing the demands of the id to be met not only realistically but morally too.

According to Freud personality is based on the dynamic interactions of these three components.

Ego:

53. The Principle of delayed gratification

This principle has been found to be essential for success. If you want to succeed at something, at some point you will need to find the ability to be disciplines and take action instead of becoming distracted and doing what is easy. Success in almost every field requires you to doing something easier(delayed gratification) in favour of doing something required and difficult.

We can train our mind to delay gratification just as we train our muscles.

****